BE KIND

It's a Mitzvah!

Kind things to say & do

You can make the world a happier place!

Naomi Shulman

illustrated by Hsinping Pan

For Lila and Stella,
who make my world a happier place

◆ ◆ ◆ ◆ ◆ ◆ ◆ ◆ ◆ ◆ ◆ ◆ ◆

The mission of Storey Publishing is to serve our customers by publishing practical information that encourages personal independence in harmony with the environment.

Edited by Deanna F. Cook and Sarah Guare
Art direction and book design by Carolyn Eckert
Text production by Jennifer Jepson Smith
Illustrations by © Hsinping Pan / Lilla Rogers Studio

Storey Publishing
210 MASS MoCA Way
North Adams, MA 01247
storey.com

Printed in China through World Print
10 9 8 7 6 5 4 3 2 1

Library of Congress Cataloging-in-Publication Data

Names: Shulman, Naomi, author.
Title: Be kind : you can make the world a happier place! : 125 kind things to say & do / by Naomi Shulman.
Description: North Adams, MA : Storey Publishing, [2019] | Audience: K to Grade 3. | Summary: "In Be Kind, kids learn that kindness is a quality that can be expressed in ways other than merely being "nice," including standing up for someone or something, engaging in a community, showing compassion toward other beings, and expressing gratitude. With joyful illustrations and kid-friendly writing, this idea book serves as a delightful, easy-to-read collection of 100 concrete activities kids and their families can pick and choose from and act out in their daily lives, whether it's being the first person to say good morning, offering compliments, shoveling an elderly neighbor's driveway, learning to say hello in different languages, or sending a card to someone —no special occasion required"— Provided by publisher.
Identifiers: LCCN 2019008885 (print) | LCCN 2019981158 (ebook) | ISBN 9781635861549 (board) | ISBN 9781635861556 (ebook) Subjects: LCSH: Kindness--Juvenile literature.
Classification: LCC BJ1533.K5 S548 2019 (print) | LCC BJ1533.K5 (ebook) | DDC 177./7--dc23
LC record available at https://lccn.loc.gov/2019008885
LC ebook record available at https://lccn.loc.gov/2019981158
062033K1/B1509/A8

WELCOME

Have you ever heard the word *mitzvah*? It means "commandment" in Hebrew, but it's often understood as a good deed. In the Torah (the first five books of the Bible) you can find 613 commandments, but there's no limit to ways of performing them. In this book, we've rounded up dozens of acts of *gemilut chasadim* ("acts of kindness") and *tikkun olam* ("repairing the world"). These are ways of being generous, compassionate, and thoughtful — not just to other people, but also to animals, the planet, and even to yourself. Give these a try! You might find that one of the great things about being kind is that it inspires even more kindness. In Hebrew, this is known as *mitzvah goreret mitzvah*: one good deed leads to another.

In the back of this book, you'll find an activity. Can you figure out which values listed there go with the actions in the book? Here's a hint: Many actions are examples of more than one value! Visit pjlibrary.org /bekind for help.

Go ahead and make kindness a habit. It's one you won't want to break.

Race to say "good morning."
Try saying it in Hebrew:
"Boker tov!"

good
morning

Learn to say
HELLO
in several languages.
You'll use the words
more than you think!

Compliment everyone —
even the cat!
Try "Nice haircut!" or

"I like your tail."

Start a conversation
with a new kid at your school:

"Hi!
MY name is ____.
What's
your name?"

Be a hug ambassador.

First:

Ask if someone wants a hug.

If the answer is yes,

Then:

Hug them!

Smile at one more person each day.

If you smile at three people today,

smile at four people

tomorrow!

If you overhear kids saying unkind things
about someone else, step in to
say something nice
about them.

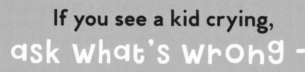

If you see a kid crying,
ask what's wrong —
and help find a grown-up
if they need one.

Paint kindness rocks.

Use nontoxic paint to add a light,
bright message on a few large rocks.
Put them somewhere
unexpected so people will get a
little surprise smile.

nice
smile

be
brave

you
rock

mazel
tov!

Share your artwork
with the world.

Make a cheerful poster,
then tape it in your window — facing out,
so people walking by will see it.

Go ahead and brag — about your friend.

Crow about their excellent grades or recent sport win.

GREAT JOB!

Be a joiner.

Is a friend putting together a quick game of basketball? Do your younger cousins want to play after dinner? Participate and add to the fun!

MAKE ROOM FOR A NEW KID

at the lunch table.

Be sure to say hi

to other kids at the lunch table.

MAKE YOUR BACKYARD A SAFE HAVEN

for winged things.

They'll bring extra joy
as they fly by your window.

Plant bird-friendly plants, like sunflowers.

Set up a bird feeder.

No bird feeder? No problem.

Make a pinecone feeder in a flash!

Tie yarn to one end of a pinecone.
Spread peanut butter all over the edges of
the pinecone, then roll it in a plate of birdseed.
Hang the coated pinecone on a tree.

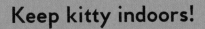

Keep kitty indoors!

Thank your
cashier or waiter.

EVERYONE APPRECIATES BEING APPRECIATED.

Put your math skills to good use:
Learn how to calculate
a generous tip.

Have a no-present night of Hanukkah.

Instead of gifts, ask your family
to donate to your favorite cause,
like an animal shelter.

Get your friends together
for a community clean-up day.
Pick up trash
around your neighborhood
(and don't forget to recycle!).

Read a book
to someone who hasn't learned how yet.

Make personalized bookmarks
for everyone in your class. Don't forget your teacher!

Check for bargains at the grocery store

and then donate some of the food
to your local food bank.

• • • • • • • • • • • • • • • • • • •

Put the grocery cart away

in the store parking lot and
take back another cart
while you're at it.
(It's actually kind of fun.)

Did someone new
move to town?
Make a welcome card
that you and
your friends sign.
Friends don't have to come from
the same place you come from.

- - - - - - - - - - - - - - - -

Have a couple of
unused ride
tickets at the fair?
Pass them on to the next kid.
Everyone deserves a
spin on a merry-go-round.

❄ SNOW DAY!

**Before you build that snow fort,
offer to shovel
a neighbor's steps.**

A warm drink is
sweeter when shared.

**If you're making a mug of
hot cocoa or tea,
make an extra serving to
deliver to a neighbor.**

Got leftovers?

Box up your untouched food and pass it along to the next homeless person you see.

Is a cold making the rounds in your neighborhood?

Leave a jar of chicken soup

and other sick-person goodies at a sniffly neighbor's house.

Slip a friendly note into another kid's backpack.

See that shy kid on the playground?

Bounce the ball her way.

Foster a pet!

Help a local animal shelter provide a temporary home for a furry friend.

♦ ♦ ♦ ♦ ♦ ♦ ♦ ♦ ♦ ♦ ♦ ♦

When your towels and blankets are threadbare, don't toss them — chances are your local animal shelter can use them.

Pet some puppies while you're there.

Make a sock toy for a cat!

Fill a small sock with catnip,
then tie the sock shut with yarn.
Leave a yarn "tail" behind.
Use a permanent marker to draw
a mouse face on the tip of the toe.

Mrs. Katz is Purrrfect!!

Write a Compliment to your teacher

on the whiteboard
when she isn't looking.
If you have enough time,
get all your classmates to sign it.

Say a sweet thank-you

to your teacher by
filling a mug with his
favorite treats.

Raining again?
Put out a bucket.
Use the collected
rainwater to water your
indoor plants.

. . . .

Carry an umbrella that's big enough for two
(or more!).

Push some little kids around – on the swings.

If you have younger neighbors,
they probably think
you are the coolest person *ever*.
Offer to play with them!
They'll have a blast,
and you'll have more fun than
you might expect.

Don't throw it — grow it!

No need to make more garbage! Instead of throwing out a sprouting potato, plant it in a pot and watch it grow.

◆ ◆ ◆ ◆ ◆ ◆ ◆ ◆ ◆ ◆ ◆

Do you have a vegetable garden?

Take some of your harvest to a local food kitchen.

Empty a glass of water into a potted plant

instead of down the sink.

Are you the dramatic type?

Take that show on the road:
Gather together some of your friends
and perform skits
at your local senior center.

Ask a senior to tell a
childhood story —
and record it!

Send a card
to your grandparents just to say  hi!

Keep a thankfulness jar.

Every single day, write down one thing you're thankful for.

. . . and when you're thankful for other people,

tell them!

See a basket of clean laundry?
FOLD IT!
Match socks if you don't know how to fold.

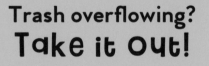

Trash overflowing?
Take it out!

Toilet paper roll empty? Replace it.

WITHOUT BEING ASKED . . .

Clean your hamster's cage.

Make your sister's bed (and your own!).

Pick up toys and clothing on the floor—
even if they're not yours.
(*Especially* if they're not yours!)

Have a screen-free day!

Giving people your
full attention is kind.
Spend a day
with the people around you —
without distractions.

Take the dog for an
extra walk.
And watch him wag his tail!

◆ ◆ ◆ ◆ ◆ ◆ ◆ ◆ ◆ ◆ ◆

On a scorching hot day,
leave a bowl of
cold water
out for animal friends.

FOUND A SPIDER?
DON'T SQUISH IT!

If it's inside,
gently catch it in a cup
and help it go outdoors.
If it's already outside,
leave it be.

Want to give tzedakah
for a cause you care about?
Organize a toy sale
with the kids on your street.
Donate the money you make from your
old toys to charity, and give
any leftovers to a charity store.

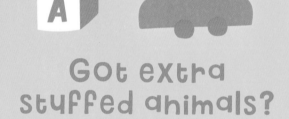

**Got extra
stuffed animals?**
Start a neighborhood
teddy bear drive. Collect gently loved
stuffed animals to donate
to a local daycare or animal shelter.

Bookworms
unite:
Leave a
nice note
(on a bookmark!)
in a library
book for the
next reader.

DONATE BOOKS
you've outgrown
to a preschool or daycare.
Pass along a PJ Library® book
to a friend!

WRITE A THANK-YOU NOTE

to local firefighters.
They're real-life superheroes.

◆ ◆ ◆ ◆ ◆ ◆ ◆ ◆ ◆ ◆

When others have
spinach in their teeth or
toilet paper stuck to their shoe,
let them know —
quietly.

Be the host with the most.

Invite people to your house,
and when they arrive, be welcoming.
Offer them a glass of water and
pull out a chair.

Learn good phone manners.

When people call, greet them
in a friendly voice and ask
what you can do to help them.

Look on the bright side!

Raining all weekend?
Perfect time to invite a friend
over and play dress-up!

Got a shot at the doctor's office?
At least you won't get sick!

There's almost always a rosy side.

Help people around you
see it, too!

Even the kindest kids
mess up sometimes.
Master the art of
saying sorry:
say it right away,
be clear about what you're
apologizing for,
and try to fix it if you can.

"I'm sorry I stepped on your flowers.
Can I help plant some new ones?"
And when someone
apologizes to you, accept it!
Forgiveness
makes everyone feel better faster.

Birthday cake only comes
around once a year.
Bake just-because
cupcakes —
and write a sweet message
on them for someone you love.

Create an in/out closet.

Got a new item of clothing?
When you put something
new IN the closet, take OUT one old item
to donate to a charity store.

◆ ◆ ◆ ◆ ◆ ◆ ◆ ◆ ◆ ◆ ◆ ◆

Has it been a loooooong time
since your last haircut?
Get it chopped, then
**donate the cut-off hair
to a charity**
that makes wigs
for sick people.

LOST & FOUND

SET UP A NEIGHBORHOOD LOST AND FOUND.

Put up signs
saying neighbors can bring
found items to your place.
When people lose something,
they can stop by and
see if anyone dropped it off.

Be the first person to
GIVE UP YOUR SEAT
to someone who needs it.

Volunteer
to make crafts at a nearby senior center!

Make friendship bracelets

for all your current pals.
Craft a few extra for the new friends
you're *going* to make.

FRIENDSHIP

Got extra art supplies?

Fill ziplock bags with
small notepads, crayons, markers,
and stickers to give out as
activity bags at a children's hospital.

When you leave an
empty room,

TURN
OFF THE
LIGHTS

and watch
the stars.

Search, Find, and Do!

Here's a list of the Jewish values described in this book. See if you can find examples of each one.

- [ ] **bal tashchit**: the mitzvah of preserving the environment
- [ ] **bikkur cholim**: the mitzvah of visiting and caring for sick people
- [ ] **chesed**: behaving kindly and lovingly toward others
- [ ] **derech eretz**: politeness, good manners
- [ ] **hachnasat orchim**: making others, especially new people, feel welcome, usually by inviting them to our home
- [ ] **hakarat hatov**: paying attention to the good in the world, showing gratitude
- [ ] **hashavat aveidah**: the mitzvah of returning lost items to their owners
- [ ] **ha'achalat re'evim**: the mitzvah of providing food to those who need it
- [ ] **kehilla**: the value of taking part in community
- [ ] **kibud zekaynim**: the mitzvah of respecting and honoring senior citizens
- [ ] **shalom bayit**: creating a sense of peacefulness and harmony in the household (or school!)
- [ ] **teshuva**: the act of repentance, saying sorry
- [ ] **tza'ar ba'alei chayim**: the mitzvah of taking care of animals
- [ ] **tikkun atzmi**: improving oneself, striving to do better
- [ ] **tikkun olam**: improving the world, working to make the world better
- [ ] **tzedakah**: the mitzvah of working to create a fair and just society, often by giving to charity

For more information on this initiative,
check us out online at
www.pjlibrary.org/organizations

To receive these resources in your inbox,
share your contact information with us at
www.pjlibrary.org/resource-reg

www.pjlibrary.org

Resource Guide

Be Kind

We understand that how we gather looks different these days. Whether you are coming together in person or online, PJ Library will continue to provide content to connect with your community. Inside you'll find ways to:

- **Creatively help each other through acts of kindness**

- **Make meaningful connections to families through Jewish values**

- **Enrich learning experiences for all ages**